WALKS ARO   YORKSHIRE COAST

10 WALKS OF 6 MILES OR LESS

Malcolm Boyes

Dalesman

First published in 2008 by Dalesman
an imprint of
Country Publications Ltd
The Water Mill
Broughton Hall
Skipton
North Yorkshire BD23 3AG

Reprinted 2016

Text © Malcolm Boyes 2008
Maps © Guelder Design & Mapping 2008
Illustrations © Christine Isherwood 2008

Cover: Flamborough by Alan Curtis

ISBN 978-1-85568-249-8

Printed in Europe for Latitude Press Ltd.

PUBLISHER'S NOTE
....
The information given in this book has been provided in good faith and is intended only
as a general guide. Whilst all reasonable efforts have been made to ensure that details
were correct at the time of publication, the author and Country Publications Ltd
cannot accept any responsibility for inaccuracies. It is the responsibility of individuals
undertaking outdoor activities to approach the activity with caution and, especially if
inexperienced, to do so under appropriate supervision. The activity described in this book
is strenuous and individuals should ensure that they are suitably fit before embarking
upon it. They should carry the appropriate equipment and maps, be properly clothed and
have adequate footwear. They should also take note of weather conditions and forecasts,
and leave notice of their intended route and estimated time of return.

Deducation
To Clive and Diane

Contents

Introduction

Between Saltburn and Bridlington lies some of the finest coastal scenery in England. The clifftop path along the eastern edge of the North York Moors National Park offers spectacular views; it forms part of the Cleveland Way long-distance footpath southwards to Filey Brigg. South of Filey the chalk Yorkshire Wolds form their last eastward thrust into the North Sea at Flamborough Head towering over the sweep of Bridlington Bay.

Nestling in the valleys are picturesque fishing villages like Robin Hood's Bay, with its narrow winding streets and lanes, and Runswick where the paths are set between gardens with colourful displays in summer. Flamborough stands on the headland, and the fishing boats were hauled out of the sea at either North or South Landing depending on the winds and tides.

While walking the clifftop paths be aware of the dangers of coastal erosion. The path may have fallen to the beach below but the local councils are always purchasing land further inland so there should be no problem in walking around the eroded part. It may be considered prudent to keep your dogs on a lead while on the clifftops. Never attempt to walk the clifftop paths in darkness. Always allow sufficient time to complete your walk before night falls.

The Yorkshire coast region regularly receives birds from continental Europe that are rare in the United Kingdom. This may be the first landfall for some hours for these birds, and they seek shelter in the shrubs and hedges along the coast to recover. The most likely times are during migration in April and May, and again in September and October. While out walking it would be worth carrying a pair of binoculars and a field guide to birds. Further information on the area's birds can be found at the RSPB centre at Bempton Cliffs (visited on walk 9). Bempton's cliffs in early summer are the breeding place of many thousands of sea birds. It is also worth carrying a field guide to wild flowers while on these walks.

The police advise that, when you leave your car to go for a walk, you ensure that no handbags or valuables are visible in the car — lock anything valuable you are not taking with you in the boot.

Saltburn & Hunt Cliff

> **Distance: 3¹/₂ miles (5.5 km)**
> **Time: 2 hours**
> **Terrain: a climb leads on to Hunt Cliff and a return is made along the coast path**
> **Start: clifftop parking in Saltburn, grid ref 665216**
> **Map: OS Explorer 306, Middlesbrough & Hartlepool**

From the clifftop in Saltburn, overlooking the pier, take the footpath indicated on the four-finger signpost 'Cleveland Way and Smugglers'. Stop at two seats which overlook the pier. On your left is the cliff railway.

Originally here was a vertical lift reached by an exposed steel walkway. The lift was replaced by the present water-powered cliff railway in 1884.

Turn right and descend the steps. At the fork, take the steps bearing right to reach the road at the foot of the steep hill. Turn left and follow the footpath as it sweeps right, away from the pier. Follow this round, to a footbridge across Skelton Beck. Pass the boats on your left, and continue along the roadside footpath to Old Saltburn nestling under Hunt Cliff. At Old Saltburn are the Ship Inn and the Saltburn Smugglers Experience.

John Andrews ran the Ship Inn from the 1780s, and he gained the title 'The King of the Smugglers'.

Follow the road to the right past the Ship Inn. Just beyond the bus stop, turn left on the stone path and immediately fork right. (The return is down the other path marked 'Cleveland Way'.) The path climbs steeply, passing the National Trust 'Old Saltburn' sign. Pass a row of houses on the left and continue on the distinct path to reach an access road to the houses. Continue straight ahead along the access road, marked as a cycle path. When the access road turns right, continue straight ahead, past a gate, along the track to Ladgates Farm. Pass the farm on the left and continue to the cottage at the end of the field. Turn left along a broad track, with views across to Saltburn.

Saltburn was created in the 1860s when the railway was extended from Redcar, by Henry Pease, a Quaker ironmaster and director of the Stockton & Darlington Railway Company, who saw its potential as a seaside resort.

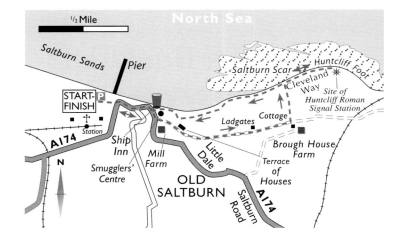

At the end of the broad path you reach the coastal path. Turn right and climb gradually for 500 yards to a stone plaque recording the site of Huntcliff Roman Signal Station.

The Roman signal station was one of a number set along the Yorkshire coast to warn of raiding pirates. (See also Walk 3.) It was built about AD 350 and destroyed about fifty years later, probably by raiding Angles as, during excavations, fourteen mutilated bodies were found in a well.

Turn back at this point and return along the clifftop path. There are panoramic views to Saltburn and the extensive sands exposed at low tide.

Saltburn Sands were used for motor racing from 1908 until the 1930s. Saltburn Speed Trials attracted top racing car drivers including S F Edge, Parry Thomas, and Malcolm Campbell and 'Bluebird'. The racing cars were brought to Saltburn on the railway using special wagons.

Pass through Hunt Cliff Nature Reserve to reach the steps which descend back to the road behind the Ship Inn. Retrace your steps back around the coast road's footpath. Just before the footbridge, look to your left along the valley, which was spanned by the Halfpenny Bridge, completed in 1869.

Continue over the footbridge you crossed earlier. At the corner there are the steps back to the start of the walk. But first you may wish to walk on Yorkshire's last remaining pier or take the cliff railway, if it is operating, up to the clifftop.

Runswick & Port Mulgrave

Distance: 4 miles (6.5 km)
Time: 2½ hours
Terrain: A steep descent and climb back out of Runswick village
Start: Runswick clifftop car park, grid ref 807161
Map: OS Explorer 27, North York Moors Eastern Area

From the entrance to the clifftop car park above Runswick, facing the Cliffmount Hotel, turn right along the old tarmac path which descends steeply to Runswick village. There are excellent views into Runswick Bay but the village lies hidden until your final approach. Take the first turn left along the flagged path between the houses and gardens. At the end, the path turns left. Take the first path left which descends some steps to reach a turning circle for cars on the right. The road to the right leads to a roundabout at the end of the steep road which descends to the lower car parks in Runswick.

It is well worth your while wandering around the paths in Runswick, and there is a hotel and places selling ice-cream. In summer the gardens are very colourful, an unusual feature in a fishing community.

Runswick's lifeboat was launched by the women of the village in March 1901, an arduous task that brought them national fame. The menfolk were out fishing when a storm blew up. A crew of older men and farm workers was gathered together, and the women lowered the lifeboat down the slipway, across the beach and far enough into the sea to float the lifeboat off its cradle. The lifeboat successfully escorted the fishing boats back into the bay. The rescue made headline news in the papers. The women were treated to a reception and dinner in Manchester, and presented with a plaque.

When you wish to leave Runswick, make your way to the mini-roundabout at the bottom of the road and turn back along the tarmac road into the village. Pass the telephone box and fork left up some steps set below the Royal Hotel. The steps lead straight up to the route you descended into the village. Turn left at the top, behind the house, and when you reach the access track turn right and climb steeply back to the car park entrance. Here you walk straight on along Bank Top Lane, passing toilets on your left.

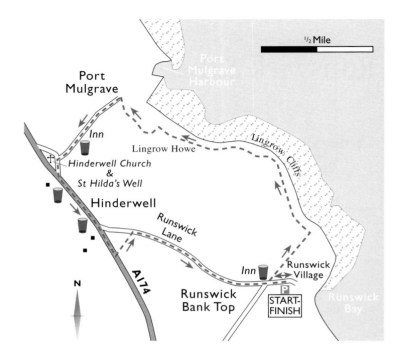

Turn right at the Runswick Bay Hotel and pass through their car park, signposted 'Cleveland Way'. A stone path with a hedge on your right and a post-and-wire fence on the left leads you through a kissing-gate on to the clifftop path. Turn left at the pond along the coast path.

The coast path was used by the villagers of Runswick in November 1924 to get a grandstand view of their rowing lifeboat Hester Rothschild *taking off the crew of nineteen from the SS* Princess Clementine *which had run ashore in heavy seas.*

The distinct path offers some magnificent views as it leads you towards the hamlet of Port Mulgrave and the harbour from which the hamlet takes its name. Just beyond the National Trust sign for Port Mulgrave, the path drops steeply down into a ravine and climbs back out. At the kissing-gate, turn left and stay on the clifftop path.

Port Mulgrave used to have a harbour, but has been eroded away over the last fifty years. It was situated where the small boats are hauled up under

A century ago the fulmar was restricted to the Scottish island of St Kilda, but is now a common sight all along the cliffed coasts of Britain and Ireland.

the cliffs. The port was built by the Grinkle Park Mining Company, which operated between 1875 and 1934. There was no road to the port. Instead, railway wagons were taken from the mine, near the site of the present Boulby Potash Mine, through tunnels to emerge at the harbour. The iron ore was loaded on to ships and taken up to Jarrow on Tyneside.

As you approach the first houses in Port Mulgrave, turn left up the road into the hamlet. The cul-de-sac road climbs steadily into Port Mulgrave. Eventually there is a footpath on the left. Pass the Ship Inn and you reach a T-junction with Hinderwell Church just visible in front of you.

The village of Hinderwell takes its name from St Hilda's Well which provided water for the community for many years. St Hilda was the abbess of the Celtic monastery at Whitby. Traditionally the local schoolchildren used to come to the well on Ascension Day, place liquorice in their bottles and fill them up with water from the well, giving the water an added taste.

Turn left along the road and walk up the steps on your right. Turn right into the churchyard. St Hilda's Well will be found behind the church along a path beside a post-and-rail fence. Retrace your steps to the churchyard entrance gate and walk straight ahead into Hinderwell. Turn left to walk through the village. You pass an old North Riding of Yorkshire mile marker set beside a wall. There are two inns in the village which may be serving drinks and meals. Many of the houses in Hinderwell have good dressed stone facades.

At the fork in the road in front of the war memorial clock, take the Whitby road on the right. Pass High Farm and use the footpath on the right. Just before the last house on your left, a footpath sign indicates a flagged path which leads to a stile into a field. Carry straight on, keeping the hedge on your left, to a stile onto a road. Turn right along the roadside footpath to Runswick. Pass the Runswick Bay Hotel and carry straight on to the Cliffmount Hotel, where you turn right into the car park.

Kettleness Point

Distance: 3¹/₂ miles (5.5 km)
Time: 2 hours
Terrain: There is a steady climb past the Roman Signal Station
into Goldsborough; field and coast paths
Start: There is limited parking around the hamlet of Kettleness
(don't block entrances), grid ref 831155
Map: OS Explorer 27, North York Moors Eastern Area

There were more people living in the village of Kettleness in the nineteenth century than there are now. Over the years alum, jet and ironstone have been extracted from the surrounding area. Alum was quarried from about 1728. On the 17th December 1829 part of the cliff collapsed and the houses slid down towards the North Sea. In the darkness the terrified inhabitants rushed from their homes and found shelter in an alum boat, waiting to be loaded with alum. Their houses and the alum works which gave them their living were destroyed. It was 1831 before the alum works reopened. There are good views of Kettleness Point where the alum was quarried on the return path into Kettleness.

From the hamlet of Kettleness, walk back along the road towards Goldsborough. On the right, pass the former railway station at Kettleness.

The railway had the grand title of the Whitby, Redcar and Middlesbrough Union Railway but was never intended to go from Whitby to either Redcar or Middlesbrough. The railway line was to be 15 miles 3 furlongs, linking existing railways at Whitby and Loftus. After leaving Kettleness for Whitby the railway entered the 308-yard (282 m) long Kettleness tunnel then, after a brief period of daylight, went into the 1,652-yard (1,510 m) long Sandsend Tunnel. The original intention had been to run the railway along a shelf cut into the cliff face. A collapse of the cliff during early work meant the directors decided to put the railway through the two tunnels. The first train ran over the line in December 1883 and the line closed in May 1958.

Continue up the road and turn left over a stile (signed 'public footpath') just before the former chapel with the ornamental slate roof. Bear right around the back of the chapel to another stile. Then climb to a gate and stile in the

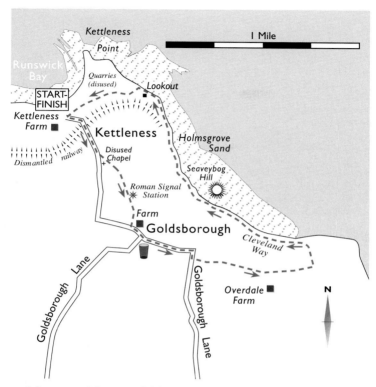

top left corner of the grass field (the track is indistinct). Cross the stile, and a plaque gives you information on the Goldsborough Roman Signal Station.

Look at the extensive view out to sea for the Romans manning this outpost. The signal station was one of five built along the Yorkshire coast to warn of seaborne raiders. The most northerly was at Hunt Cliff above Saltburn (see Walk 1). Heading south, the signal stations were here at Goldsborough, Ravenscar, on the site of the Raven Hall Hotel (see Walk 4), Scarborough Castle Headland and Filey Brigg. If raiders were seen, the warning beacon was lit and this would be seen by the other signal stations, alerting soldiers who could be brought to the site of any landing.

Continue upwards, walking across the grass field, to a gate and stile in the opposite corner. The buildings in the village of Goldsborough can be seen on the skyline. A signpost acts as a guide. Cross the stile and continue to another stile beside a gate, where you enter the farmyard. Bear right around the building and a metal gate gives access to the road. Turn left through Goldsborough. At the road junction, carry straight on along the road signposted 'Lythe and Whitby'. Pass a telephone box on your right, and on your left some corrugated iron which covers the quoits pitches.

A quoit is a metal ring weighing about 5^1/$_4$ pounds (2.5 kg). The aim of the game is to throw the ring over a peg which is beneath the covers. Other variations of the throw are to place your ring against the peg to stop your opponent placing his quoit over the peg.

Dune pansies are a colourful addition to sandy stretches of the coast.

Pass the Fox and Hounds Inn on your right and continue down the road. After quarter of a mile the road turns right and in fifty yards you turn left, at the public bridleway sign, along the stone access road to Overdale Farm. Ahead are views along the coast to the harbour arms at Whitby jutting into the North Sea. To the right you can see the squat spire of Lythe Church.

When the access track turns right to Overdale Farm, carry straight on, signposted 'Sandsend', keeping a stunted hedge on your left. At the T-junction turn left to the coast path where you can see a signpost. At the signpost turn left ('Kettleness 1.5 miles') and follow the coast path. This is part of the Cleveland Way long-distance footpath. As you walk towards Kettleness, keep to the coast path — don't follow any tractor tracks inland. Eventually you get excellent views down on to Kettleness Point, which was quarried for alum.

Kettleness Point was believed to deflect ships' compasses, due to the ironstone in the area. The villagers of Runswick, across the bay, were always willing to stop their fishing to help offload the cargo of a ship to help it refloat at high tide. This was often done with the blessing of the insurers who got free labour. Unloading colliers (coal was a regular part of the coastal trade) was dirty work. The fishermen worked in relays, taking the coal ashore to a safe place. One villager never bought any coal from 1911 until well into the 1930s.

The coast path leads back into Kettleness.

Robin Hood's Bay

Distance; 3¹/₄ miles (5 km)
Time: 1¹/₂ hours
Terrain: An easy walk along well-defined paths with one climb
from the coast path to the former railway line for the return walk
Start: large car park in Robin Hood's Bay (charge, free in winter),
grid ref 950054
Map: OS Explorer 27, North York Moors Eastern Area

The large car park stands on the site of the railway station at Robin Hood's Bay. The influx of a large number of navvies to build the railway in the early 1880s did cause problems. The Scarborough Gazette *of 24th April 1884 reported that a number of navvies who had been drinking then quarrelled and a fight ensued. The police were called and the navvies started fighting the police. Eventually the police, with the help of some civilians, broke up the fight and three navvies were arrested. A number of people were injured.*

From the car park walk down to the entrance and take the road on your left — Mount Pleasant North, signposted as a cycle path and part of the Cleveland Way. At the end of Mount Pleasant North, walk straight on through a wooden gate, signposted 'Cleveland Way'. Walk along a stone path with houses and gardens to your left. Pass through a gate and take the field path to the right along the edge of Rocket Post Field, indicated by a National Trust sign. Follow the post-and-wire fence on your left.

You can see the rocket post, where the field gets its name, at the end of the field. Beside the path is an information board giving details of the rocket post's use. A nearby seat offers excellent views into Robin Hood's Bay.

The bay was the scene of a dramatic rescue in 1881. Mr Trueman Robinson of Robin Hood's Bay owned the Visitor, *a 58-year-old brig operating as a collier between Tyneside and London. It was caught in a storm off Flamborough Head and blown north into Robin Hood's Bay. On the 19th January the crew abandoned the ship when it had five feet of water in the hold and took to the lifeboat, sheltering in the lee of the boat. Shortly afterwards the boat sank, but still offered protection to the crew in the lifeboat. The Whitby lifeboat was called at first light but, due to the storm,*

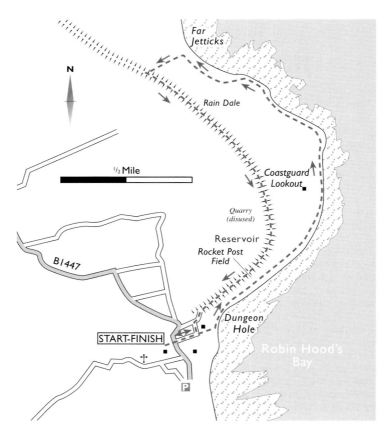

it was impossible for it to be rowed out of the harbour. The dramatic decision was taken — "We'll launch from Bay". This involved dragging the lifeboat eight miles (13 km) on its cradle over the snow-covered roads, with drifts up to seven feet, and descending through the narrow streets of the village to launch the lifeboat. Sixty people and eleven horses began to haul the boat overland. Meanwhile another group began cutting a path out of Robin Hood's Bay. By 1.30pm the lifeboat was ready to launch. On the first attempt to reach the sailors, the lifeboat was hit by a massive wave which broke six of the oars. Returning to the village, two injured lifeboatmen were removed, new oars found, and with a crew of eighteen the lifeboat successfully reached the six crew of the *Visitor* and brought them ashore.

The black-headed gull is the most common gull of the English coast.

Continue walking to the end of Rocket Post Field and turn left on the coast path. Cross over a small stone footbridge with steps at either side. As you walk along the clifftop path you will see a white wooden-topped coastguard lookout station on your left across the field. You pass a gate with access to a conservation area on your left above Cow and Calf Rocks.

This path is the first, or more accurately the last, section of the Coast to Coast Walk devised by Alfred Wainwright. The other end of the walk is at St Bees in Cumbria. The 190-mile (305 km) walk passes through the Lake District, the Yorkshire Dales and North York Moors national parks to terminate at the slipway in Robin Hood's Bay.

At the top of the next rise there are good views of the cliffs rising over 200 feet (60 m) above the North Sea. Cross two wooden bridges across small streams. The coast path climbs to a signpost indicating on the left 'To Railway Path'. Turn left here. The grass path climbs steeply. Keep the drystone wall on your left. As you near the top the path bears right, away from the drystone wall, to a gate onto the former railway line. Pause here and look at the excellent sea views. Turn left along the former track of the Scarborough to Whitby Railway.

There are good views from the former railway track, looking down on the route you walked earlier and out to sea. After one and a quarter miles (2 km) of pleasant, easy walking you approach the houses of Robin Hood's Bay. Turn left at the signpost and pass some garages on your right. At the bottom, turn right where there is a Cleveland Way and Railway Path sign. Walk back along Mount Pleasant North and cross the road to the car park entrance.

Don't forget to walk down into Robin Hood's Bay. The steep footpath beside the equally steep road descends among the closely crammed houses. (Imagine the problems in lowering a lifeboat around these tight corners.) The village offers all you will need, with three inns and several shops.

15

The Alum Coast

Distance: 4½ miles (7km)
Time: 2½ hours
Terrain: good paths which are well signposted, but a steep climb
from Stoupebrow Cottage Farm to the disused railway track
Start: the long roadside car park in Ravenscar, grid ref 980015
Map: OS Explorer 27, North York Moors Eastern Area

From the car park, opposite the toilets, there are extensive views into Robin Hood's Bay. The village of Robin Hood's Bay can be seen across the bay: the older part, where the houses crowd together, is set in the ravine; the newer part stands on the more level area above the ravine. The Raven Hall Hotel in Ravenscar stands on the site of a former Roman Signal Station (see Walk 3). Ravenscar used to be called Peak.

Walk down to the entrance of the Raven Hall Hotel and turn left, down Peakside, along the concrete road. On your right is the National Trust centre where you can obtain information on the National Trust's activities in the area and on the local alum trade. Continue down the concrete path and along the one signposted 'Cleveland Way and National Trust, Peak Alum Works'.

If you look at the bricks set in the path you will see the word 'Ravenscar' fired into them. The bricks were produced at Whitakers brickworks, situated in the Peak Alum Quarries which scar the hillside to your left. The brickworks opened about 1900 and closed about 1939.

Ignore the fork to the right which leads to the former railway. Continue walking along the Cleveland Way. The distinct path forks right and continues descending. Keep following the Cleveland Way and eventually you reach a junction. On the right you see a signpost, 'Alum Works Only'. Take this National Trust permissive path which allows access to the former Peak Alum Works. There is a warning notice of an adder colony in the area, but it is doubtful if you will see any — they usually move away on your approach.

Alum was quarried in North Yorkshire for about 300 years up to the end of the nineteenth century. Alum was a valuable chemical used in fixing colours

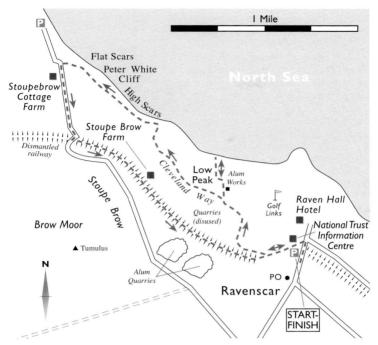

1 Mile

Flat Scars
Peter White
Cliff

North Sea

Stoupebrow
Cottage
Farm

High Scars

Stoupe Brow
Farm

Dismantled
railway

Cleveland Way

Low
Peak

Alum
Works

Stoupe Brow

Brow Moor

Raven Hall
Hotel

Golf
Links

Quarries
(disused)

National Trust
Information
Centre

▲ Tumulus

N

Alum
Quarries

PO ●

Ravenscar

START-
FINISH

when dyeing cloth, and in the paper and leather manufacturing industries. The alum was burnt in massive piles layered with brushwood. The resulting shale was brought down to the alum works. Here it was steeped in pits, and the resulting liquid was mixed with an alkali to enable it to crystallise. The alkali was obtained by burning seaweed and human urine which was bought in bulk in London for ten shilling (50p) a ton. It was brought in the ships coming to take the alum away. The scenery surrounding the works may be spectacular, but the smell would have been noxious! On the site, information boards detail the purposes of the various buildings and the place where the alum was lowered to waiting boats beneath the cliffs.

Return back to the Cleveland Way, turning right on the broad path to continue to Stoupebrow Cottage Farm. Turn right at the gate and Cleveland Way sign. Turn left at the end of the field. Continue to follow the distinct path with a wire-and-post fence on your left. There are wonderful coastal views into Robin Hood's Bay. Cross a footbridge and turn right along the coast path. On the hillside to your left you can see the quarries where the alum was extracted. Cross a footbridge to reach a Second World War

17

pillbox. The path continues over stiles to reach the road near Stoupebrow Cottage Farm. Turn left and begin the steep ascent on this quiet cul-de-sac road. Pause on the way to admire the excellent scenery behind you.

The road was at one time the main road into Robin Hood's Bay from the south. There was a steep descent to the beach and the horse-drawn coaches then crossed the sands to reach the village.

The cinnabar moth, with its distinctive red and grey wings, is usually seen in small groups in coastal areas.

At the top of the climb, the road turns two bends. A broad track on your left leads to the former railway track of the Scarborough to Whitby Railway. (If you reach the road bridge over the railway you have passed the turn.) Turn left along the former railway line which offers spectacular views into Robin Hood's Bay and across to the castellated walled gardens of the Raven Hall Hotel. Approaching Ravenscar, formerly the route turned left before a railway tunnel.

The cheapest option for the builders of the railway line would have been to make a cutting. W H Hammond of the Raven Hall Hotel strongly objected and insisted on a 279-yard (255 m) long tunnel. The tunnel was built in 1876, then found to be on the wrong alignment and had to be rebuilt in 1883. It cost £500. W H Hammond died in 1885. The railway line opened on 16th July 1885, and it closed on the 6th March 1965 under the Beeching Plan to rationalise the railways, It was the end of one of the most scenic lines in Britain.

At the time of writing the path has been diverted along a well-signposted diversion due to a landslip. The path turns right at a wooden barrier off the former railway, circling round to run parallel below the railway line. Eventually the distinct track rejoins the Cleveland Way which you walked down earlier. The buildings of Ravenscar can be seen ahead and above you. Climb back up to the road in Ravenscar and turn right to the car park, where you can look back over your scenic route.

Walk 6

Hayburn Wyke

Distance: 2³/₄ miles (4.5 km)
Time: 1¹/₂ hours
Terrain: easy route-finding along a well-signposted coast path
with a return along a disused railway track
Start: limited parking in Hood Lane off the Cloughton to
Ravenscar road, grid ref 014955
Map: OS Explorer 27, North York Moors Eastern Area

Having parked in Hood Lane, walk along the road towards the coast and pass under the railway bridge which carried the former Scarborough to Whitby railway over the lane. When the tarmac ends, near the houses, fork left up the broad track, At the top there are extensive views south.

Looking south you can see Scarborough Castle's keep standing prominently on the headland. The headland was the site of a Roman signal station, one of a series built along the Yorkshire Coast to warn of raiders. (See walks 1, 3 and 4.)

The lane eventually becomes a grass track signposted as a public footpath which continues to the coast path. On your right there is a seat with excellent views both south and out into the North Sea.

The coastal shipping during the First World War was in danger of being hit by both German submarines and mines. On the 6th June 1917 the 2,294 ton SNA II *was torpedoed off this stretch of coast and just over two months later on the 24th August the SS* Springhill *hit a mine.*

Your route north is along the signposted Cleveland Way. It is a field-side path with the clifftop on your right beyond the hawthorn hedge. As you begin to descend towards Hayburn Wyke, you can see down to the small, quiet cove where a small waterfall drops on to the beach.

Smuggling was rife along the Yorkshire coast and probably reached its peak towards the end of the nineteenth century. The activity involved all members of society, from the gentry who financed the buying of the goods, the fishermen who brought the contraband ashore, the labourers who quickly

19

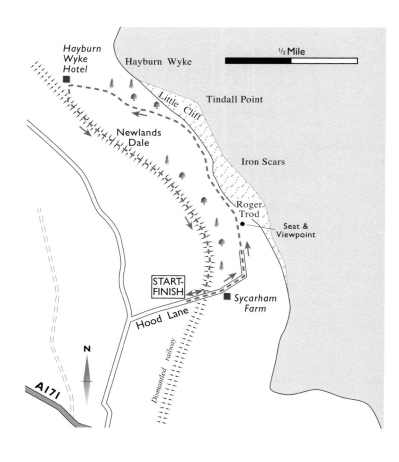

offloaded the boats and took the smuggled goods to secret depositories, the pannier men and carters who moved the goods inland or to the coastal towns and the shopkeepers who resold the goods. It wasn't just brandy and gin that was smuggled — anything that was highly taxed came ashore. The goods being offloaded from a coble could include silk, playing cards, chocolate, tea, snuff and spinning wheels.

Eventually the coast path descends stone steps into a deciduous wood. At this point there is a National Trust sign indicating Hayburn Wyke land.

20

The woods are a nature reserve. The trees are a mixture of oak, ash, hazel and chestnut, and even some walnut trees. The woodland provides a haven for birds. There is a chance you may see pied flycatcher, chaffinch, blackcap, and greater spotted woodpecker. Also listen for the distinctive call of the chiffchaff.

After a short descent you turn left, where the Cleveland Way sign indicates a turn to the right for the Cleveland

Keep an eye out for the diminutive treecreeper in Hayburn Wyke woods.

Way to continue to Ravenscar and Whitby. Your path through the woods soon leads to a stile beside a gate which passes into a grass field. Bear right across the field to a gate which leads into a lane. Turn right. The lane leads to the Hayburn Wyke Hotel and the site of the former station on the Scarborough to Whitby Railway.

Hayburn Wyke Station must have been an excellent place to work, with only about ten trains a day. Not all trains stopped here, and one engine driver who made an unscheduled stop was told to read his working timetable.

Your route back turns sharp left along a tarmac road as you approach the hotel. Turn left at the ornate National Cycle Network sign indicating 8.5 miles to Scarborough. Your route back is through the gate and along the former Scarborough to Whitby railway line.

The tree-lined avenue offers occasional views to the coast on your left. As the peaceful valley on your left flattens out, you can see Scarborough Castle keep again. After a mile of easy, pleasant walking you cross over the bridge over Hood Lane. Forty yards beyond the bridge, turn left, and a distinct path descends beside a wire fence to the road. Turn left under the bridge back to your parking place.

Cloughton Wyke

> **Distance: 4¹/₂ miles (7 km)**
> **Time: 2¹/₂ hours**
> **Terrain: there are four climbs up steps along the coast path;**
> **the return is made on the disused railway track**
> **Start: there is a small car park at Cloughton Wyke, grid ref**
> **018952; alternatively you can undertake the walk from Crook**
> **Ness car park, grid ref 025935, and read the walk from the**
> **paragraph marked 'alternative start point'**
> **Map: OS Explorer 27, North York Moors Eastern Area**

From the car park at Cloughton Wyke, walk down, past the seat, and descend some steps to the coast path. Turn right, passing a post-and-rail fence, and climb a series of steps. At the top, carry straight on with a field on your right, then fork left at the acorn sign on the distinct path. Keep a hedge on your left and a post-and-rail fence on your right. There are good views across Cloughton Wyke to Hundale Point. The path descends a series of steps into a ravine and steps climb out again.

You can see massive boulders that have been brought down by coastal erosion at the foot of the cliffs.

As you follow the clifftop path you climb four series of steps between Cloughton Wyke and Crook Ness. Approaching Hundale Point, descend the next steps to a footbridge and stone steps lead out.

Hundale Point was the scene of a rescue by the Burniston Rocket Brigade. On 6th December 1894 the 1,234 ton steam schooner Richmond *en route from Rotterdam to the River Tyne ran aground beneath Hundale Point. At the time she was travelling at about seven knots and stranded in an upright position. The crew were all rescued by the rocket brigade. The captain and part-owner of the boat, Thomas Leinster, had absconded while awaiting trial on a charge of setting fire to the boat eight months earlier.*

The fourth set of stone steps leads to a field-side path. Continue walking along the clifftop towards the white wooden hut which is visible on the clifftop.

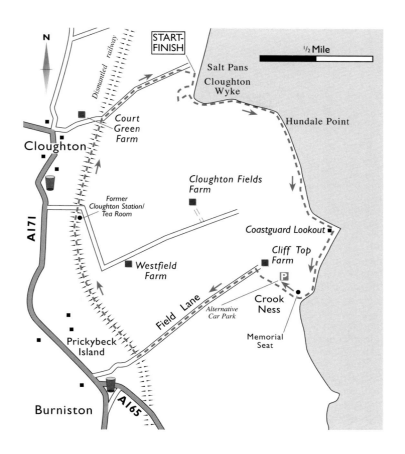

The white wooden hut was the coastguard lookout station at Long Nab. From this point there is an extensive marine view. It was erected in 1927 to maintain a watch on passing coastal traffic during bad weather. During the Second World War it was manned twenty-four hours a day by two men. The brick-built shelter to the north was to provide protection if the lookout station was attacked by enemy aircraft. The station closed in 1992 and is now used by the local ornithological group.

Continue along the clifftop path with wide-ranging views around you. At a seat the path turns inland to avoid the sheer descent into Crook Ness.

Sea campion.

The seat was erected by National Park Rangers in memory of Peter Gough, team leader of the Scarborough and District Search & Rescue Team, and a close friend of mine.

Follow the path round to the road and car park. Ignore the steps and signposted route on your left where the Cleveland Way carries on south to Scarborough.

Walk down the cul-de-sac road from Crook Ness car park *(alternative start point)*. At the T-junction near Cliff Top Farm, turn left towards the village of Burniston. The road has broad grass verges and seats, and a variety of birds may be seen as you walk along. Pass under the former railway bridge on the Scarborough to Whitby railway line. Turn left and climb some stone steps to the former railway track, and turn left across the bridge, There are pleasant views westwards to the villages of Burniston and Cloughton as you walk along the former railway track.

Burniston was the home of William Mead who had taken part in smuggling activities. He turned king's evidence and denounced some of his former smuggling friends. Locals returning from Scarborough would sing derogatory ditties under his window, until one night William Mead flung open the window and fired at the group, killing a farmer.

As you approach the old railway station at Cloughton, notice a railway carriage on your right. The former stone-built station now provides teas and accommodation. Pass the station on your right where a side line ran to a cattle dock and goods shed. One of the old station lamps can be seen on the right.

At the road, turn right for twenty yards, then turn left through a gate back onto the former railway track where there is a National Cycle Network sign. Continue along the track until you pass under a stone roadbridge. Turn left up a set of steps. At the top, turn left across the bridge and continue down the quiet road back to the car park at Cloughton Wyke.

24

Filey Brigg

Distance: 4¹/₂ miles (7 km)
Time: 2¹/₂ hours
Terrain: field paths and a clifftop walk
**Start: North Cliff Country Park, Filey (charge for parking,
free in winter), grid ref 118812**
Map: OS Explorer 301, Scarborough & Bridlington

Park at the lower end of the North Cliff Country Park, near the ticket machine. Walk back through the entrance along the footpath and take the second turn right to the roundabout. Take the Scarborough road on the right. At the end of the houses on your right there is a public footpath sign indicating your route to the clifftop path. Turn right here and the lane becomes a field path. It swings left, then right. Continue across the fields with a ditch on the left. When the ditch ends, continue straight ahead to reach the clifftop path with rugged coastal scenery beyond. Turn right along the clifftop path.

From your high vantage point you can look right into Filey, nestling under these cliffs to the north for protection. Ahead is Filey Brigg, the headland jutting out into the North Sea, and the scene of many shipwrecks. One of the earliest recorded was in 1542 when the Scottish barque Martin *was driven on to the Brigg in a storm. The local people managed to salvage wool, fish, cloth and some money for their own use. During the First World War the area was plagued by German submarines and a number of ships were torpedoed. The 1,274-ton steamer* Ardens *was torpedoed off Filey Brigg on 18th August 1917; in June 1917 she had avoided a torpedo fired at her, and earlier she had sunk a U-Boat with her bow gun.*

Continue walking along the clifftop path, and on your right you will see a post in the middle of the field with notched steps at the side. This is a rocket pole used for practice by the Filey Volunteer Life Saving Rocket Company.

The Filey Volunteer Life Saving Rocket Company operated between 1872 and the 1960s, when helicopters and other means were employed to remove shipwrecked sailors from their wrecks. The Rocket Company would attempt to fire rockets from the clifftop across the shipwreck, then a breeches buoy

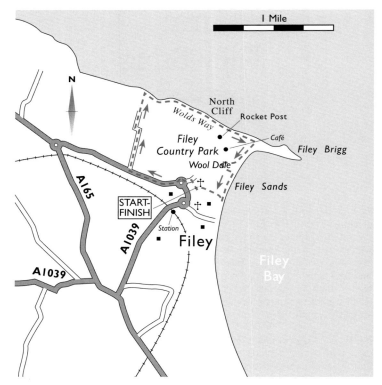

system could be used to bring the crew ashore. No easy feat when a gale was blowing. In March 1916 HMS Mekong *ran ashore near Gristhorpe. The Rocket Company managed to bring the crew ashore, but not before one man lost his life trying to swim ashore with a line.*

As you approach Filey Brigg the route forks right to a stone sculpture commemorating the ends of the Cleveland Way and Wolds Way footpaths. (You have just walked the last mile of the Cleveland Way.) The path continues past a pond on your right to a five-barred gate which gives access into North Cliff Country Park.

Walk down the tarmac path ahead of you which swings right to a café. Opposite the café, descend the road beyond the five-barred gate marked 'Filey Sailing Club'. The small valley is well wooded and provides a haven for migrating birds. At the bottom you reach the beach in Filey Bay.

You may spot a common seal on one of these walks, particularly in sheltered waters.

Filey Bay is believed to be the last resting place of the Bonhomme Richard, *John Paul Jones's ship which was destroyed in the Battle of Flamborough Head (see Walk 10).*

Turn right when you reach the beach, along the sands, to Coble Landing where Filey's fishing cobles are stored. Continue ahead to the road junction and turn right. In a few yards, just beyond the telephone box, turn right up the steps. Walk along the path which climbs the side of the wooded ravine. At the top, turn left and follow the tarmac path towards the stone boundary wall of St Oswald's churchyard.

The most famous vicar of Filey was Canon Arthur Neville Cooper who was known as the Walking Parson. He was born in 1850 and was vicar of Filey for fifty-five years. He completed a walk from Filey to London, setting out after his Sunday evening service and returning from London by train to take the following Sunday morning service. On one occasion he completed a 741-mile (1,185 km) walk to Rome in six weeks. On another occasion he walked the 653 miles (1,045 km) to Venice. He wrote a number of popular books about his adventures. Canon Cooper died aged ninety-three. There is a gravestone and plaque to him in the church sanctuary.

At the end of the path, near the church entrance, descend slightly towards a footbridge giving access to the oldest part of Filey and the town centre. Don't cross the bridge but take the tarmac path to the right and climb slightly to a road. Cross to the footpath on your right. When you reach a stone path on the right, walk along this and turn right back into North Cliff Country Park.

Walk 9

Bempton Cliffs

Distance: 4³/₄ miles (8 km)
Time: 2¹/₂ hours
Terrain: a clifftop walk, field paths and then roadside paths
Start: Bempton Cliffs, RSPB car park (charge, free to RSPB members), grid ref 197739
Map: OS Explorer 301, Scarborough & Bridlington

From the car park, walk across to the RSPB Centre and leave through the door opposite, where there is usually a list of birds seen in the area recently. (If the centre is closed, access to the field path to the cliffs can be gained through a wooden door near the toilets.) Walk out of the centre to the fork in the chalk path. The path back to the left leads to a bird-feeding station which may help you identify birds seen on the walk later in the day. Our walk takes the path to the right which passes along the edge of the field, to reach the clifftop path. Turn left at the signpost along the path 'Headland Way to Speeton'. After walking seventy yards there is a viewing area on your right where you can look out onto the chalk cliffs with its numerous ledges which are the breeding ground of thousands of seabirds.

Bempton Cliffs is the largest concentration of breeding seabirds on the English mainland, and it is the only mainland site for breeding gannets — these white birds with black wing-tips and a yellow head are seen most dramatically when they dive into the sea after fish. The most common bird is the kittiwake with its distinctive call, which can reach over 75,000 pairs. Looking down on the cliff shelves you will see common guillemots (black bird with white underside and a pointed bill) and razorbills (similarly black and white with a broader bill). The stars of this show are the puffins with their distinctive red bills. Other birds likely to be seen around the cliffs include herring gulls, fulmars and jackdaws.

Gannet.

28

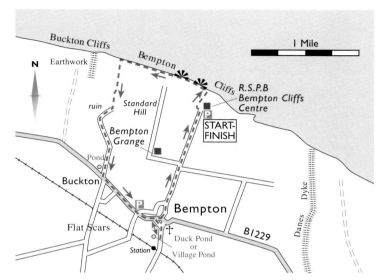

Continue walking along the clifftop path. The next viewing area has spectacular views south-eastwards to Flamborough Head with a succession of headlands jutting out into the North Sea.

It may be difficult to believe, but for centuries local men were lowered over the cliffs on ropes to gather seabird eggs. The first Bird Protection Act was passed in 1869 to protect these birds. Bird-egg collecting was made illegal in 1954, and since then the bird colonies have increased dramatically.

Continue walking along the clifftop. On the hillside on your left are the remains of a Second World War radar station.

In the 1920s there were experiments with death rays to try to stop enemy aircraft. That proved a false hope but Robert Watson-Watt, who was head of the radio section of the National Physical Laboratory, developed a system of detecting aircraft. The distinctive outline of Flamborough Head was used by German bomber crews to fix their position as they crossed the coast heading for the inland industrial cities of the North. There was a series of these radar stations all around Britain warning of incoming enemy aircraft and alerting RAF fighter stations.

One mile after beginning your clifftop walk, reach a signpost indicating a field path on the left to Buckton. Take the grassy path, keeping the wire

29

Bempton Cliffs.

fence on your right. After half a mile you reach a stile where a signpost points back to the cliffs. Cross the stile and turn left to another stile which gives access into Hoddy Cows Lane. Turn right after the stile and the grassy lane is signposted 'Footpath to Buckton'. Pass a small pond on your right and continue past gorse bushes to a kissing gate beside a five-barred gate. Your route leads down eventually to the Flamborough-Speeton coast road where there is a pond on the right with an island home for ducks.

The hedges and bushes in Hoddy Cows Lane are an excellent place to find migrating birds in April and May when they have arrived from the continent, and in September and October when they return and other Scandinavian birds fly in to overwinter. These include wagtails, common and black redstarts, various warblers, northern wheatears and spotted and pied flycatchers.

Turn left on the footpath beside the road passing through Buckton and into Bempton. At the crossroads, at the White Horse Inn, the road to the right leads down to Bempton's thirteenth-century church. Just beyond, on the right, is Bempton village green with a pond (containing Canada Geese when I last visited) and an old, restored, water pump. Return to the crossroads and take the road opposite, signposted 'RSPB Bempton Cliffs'. At the first road to the left is a plaque recording that there was a whalebone arch at this point.

Whalebone was brought back from the Arctic by the whaling boats operating out of Whitby and Hull. It had numerous uses including stiffening for corsets, grilles and even beds were made from the bones. A ship returning to port full would hang a pair of whalebones from the masthead. Some ships were unsuccessful and returned nearly empty, and others never returned from these cold, stormy waters.

The road leads straight back to the RSPB car park. While it is a narrow road with passing places, there is a broad grass verge where you can safely walk.

Flamborough Head

Distance: 6 miles (9.5 km)
Time: 3 hours
Terrain: field paths and a clifftop walk with two sections of road walking
Start: street parking in Flamborough village, grid ref 226705
Map: OS Explorer 301, Scarborough & Bridlington

Flamborough village was a fishing community with two harbours, North Landing and South Landing, giving the fishermen a choice of where to land their cobles (small fishing boats) in bad weather. Beside the roundabout are two memorials to those who lost their lives on the rugged coast.

From the roundabout in Flamborough village, walk down Post Office Street. Pass the Ship Inn and turn left along the street, then turn right along School Lane (the sign for School Lane is on the building on the right). Continue straight ahead past the 'no entry' signs and continue to the junction. Bear slightly right to the Stylefield Road sign. At the end of the cul-de-sac, a stile gives access to a field path.

The footpath is signposted 'Footpath to the Lighthouse'. Don't be put off by the distance — it is wrong. Steps descend to a field path. Keep the hedge on your left to reach a footbridge over a stream. Continue straight ahead and follow the field edge when it turns right to reach a kissing-gate which gives access to the Flamborough Village to Headland road. Turn left along the roadside footpath for about a mile.

Thirty yards beyond the 30mph speed limit sign, turn right over a footbridge and descend a set of steps, signposted 'New Fall'. Continue straight ahead, keeping the hedge on your left. Pass the edge of Old Fall Plantation, where there is a small nature trail, and eventually you will reach the clifftop path. There are extensive views of Bridlington Bay.

Turn left along the clifftop path. Flamborough Lighthouse, where you are heading, can be seen in the distance. After three-quarters of a mile, the path eventually splits. Turn left, but in ten yards fork right along a path between a hedge and a wire fence. When you reach the tarmac path, turn left and

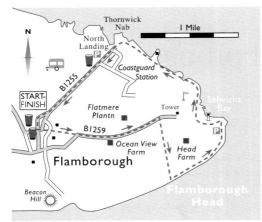

follow the brick perimeter wall of the lighthouse round to an area with seats and a toposcope, where there are exceptional views into Selwicks Bay. Behind you are shops, toilets and a café.

Nearby is a plaque recording the Battle of Flamborough Head which took place on 23rd September 1779. The battle took place at night and was witnessed by many people on the headland. John Paul Jones, working for the Americans after their Declaration of Independence, attacked a fleet of forty-three ships off Flamborough Head. Two English frigates, the Serapis *and the* Countess of Scarborough, *attacked Jones's ship the* Bonhomme Richard *and sank it, but Jones had already captured the* Serapis, *transferred his crew to it and escaped. Also nearby is an iron beacon erected to celebrate the 400th anniversary of the defeat of the Spanish Armada.*

Walk along the road beyond the Armada Beacon and turn right along a signposted path to North Landing. Pass through a gate and follow a rough tarmac path, then pass a wire fence and turn left along the distinct path which climbs to a World War II pillbox. Looking inland, you can see the original chalk beacon lighthouse built in 1674. Continue along the easy-to-follow clifftop path, with a golf course on the left, eventually passing above North Landing.

Looking across the bay, you can see a number of caves in the cliffs. It is rumoured that some of the caves around Flamborough Head were used to store smuggled goods. One of the caves is called Robin Lythe's Hole, after a character in Mary Anerley, *a tale of smuggling set around Flamborough, written by R D Blackmore, more famous for his novel* Lorna Doone.

Descend into a small ravine and climb up to the large building (a café). Take the footpath beside the road back to Flamborough village. When the road bears right to Bridlington, carry straight on into Flamborough village centre and turn right at the Ship Inn back to the roundabout.